Time to Heal

Also by Alexandra Vasiliu

Dare to Let Go
Healing Is a Gift
Be My Moon
Healing Words
Magnetic
Blooming
Through the Heart's Eyes
Plant Hope

Time to Heal

Poems
for Those Who Feel Broken and Lost

Alexandra Vasiliu

Stairway Books
2022

For permission requests, please contact Alexandra Vasiliu at Stairway
Books, 3324 E Ray Rd #1228, Higley, AZ 85236, or at
alexandra@alexandravasiliu.net.

Time to Heal*: Poems for Those Who Feel Broken and Lost* by Alexandra
Vasiliu. Stairway Books, 2022
ISBN-13: 9798361494057
First US paperback edition, November 2022

Editing services: Melanie Underwood at www.melanieunderwood.co.uk
Cover Illustration: Elena Barenbaum via www.shutterstock.com
Book Illustrations: Simple Line via www.shutterstock.com

For all those who want to heal and reclaim their lives

Contents

Time to Heal

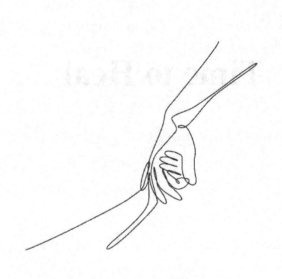

Slowly, Heal

If your heart is crushed,
don't spend your time crying,
complaining,
acting like a victim,
and becoming bitter.
Don't treat your suffering
as an intruder,
but instead as a fabulous teacher.
It is time to heal your precious self.
Convert your pain into wisdom.
Bring simplicity and peace back
into your life.
Slowly heal your heart.
There is no turning back
for you now.
You will grow through healing,

and that is one of the greatest things
in life.
Be gentle and firm
and always remind yourself,
There is no life wrecked beyond repair.

A Narrow Exit

There is no map for a broken heart.
Where to go?
Where to escape?
There are no destinations
for a half-dead heart.
Where to run?
There are no bridges higher than grief.
Now,
you realize
there is no map
that can help a broken heart
to find a way to live again.
You are trapped inside.
Now,
you live
in the most pessimistic

and dangerous place
on earth –
your deep wounds.
Take a deep breath.
Wipe your tears.
Let me show you a tiny, narrow exit –
it is a healing journey.
Your healing journey.
A unique and profound way
that is meant to help you
and any other broken heart
to get back home.
Back to your innocent self
and young dreams.
Embrace this remarkable journey
and make room for my poetry book
in your heart.
I hope
you will feel better.
I hope
you will heal.

Learning

In this life,
we are all perpetual students,
learning one lesson:
how to love
in a pure way.
No dramas.
No traumas.
No cries.
No betrayals.
To learn this excellent lesson of love,
we only need to be awake spiritually
and tirelessly heal ourselves.

Come In

If you want to heal your hidden wounds,
you will come back
to your vulnerable self.
You will knock at your soul's door
and ask permission to enter.

To your surprise,
you will never hear,
'Who is it?'
Your soul will never ask you
and never need a second guess.
Your soul will already know
that you returned home.
You will enjoy a warm welcome,
'Come in, dear!
I have waited for you for so long.
Come in.
Make yourself comfortable.
We will share this inner space
for the rest of our lives,
so let's strive to heal.
Let's try to turn every pain into wisdom.
One day,
we can be happy again.'

A Wonderful Soul

In a self-obsessed society
where the image of your body
means everything,
turn your eyes inward
and give all your attention to your soul,
to your spiritual and emotional needs.
You are not only your body;
free yourself from this bias.
You are mainly your soul.
A wonderful, unique soul.
Whenever you want
to start your healing journey,
remind yourself
that your soul envelops your body,
and you are not just a heart
carried in the flesh.

Be Awake

There is no greater gift
than being awake
while you travel through life –
this vast field of joys and sorrows.
Cultivate self-consciousness,
open the eyes of your heart,
nourish your psyche with peace,
and your inner child with kindness.
When you encounter brokenness,
try to heal it.
When you meet happiness,
try to spread it.
There is no other reward
in this journey
than becoming
a helper of God.

Alexandra Vasiliu

To the One Who Left You

If your loved one shows you
emotional disengagement
and finally leaves you,
you will feel rejected,
uninterested,
and unwanted.

Start slowly to accept
the painful ending of your relationship.
Don't allow yourself
to feel emotionally withdrawn.
You can't change anything that happened,
but you can change
how you think about yourself.
Take the time to heal
your emotional wounds.
Take the time
to clarify your mind
and purify your heart.
Take all the time in the world
to reconnect with yourself,
to understand your hidden self,
and love yourself wisely.
Take all the time you need
to find your own way
to change
and grow positively.
Take all the time you need
to forgive the past.
Slowly, but steadily,
you will discover many innate skills
that help you recover.

You will find
how precious you truly are.
You will feel loved and valued.
And one day,
when you look into the mirror,
you will have the courage
to tell the ghost of your loved one,
'I forgave you.
I am more alive and awake than you.
I am healed now.
I am no longer yours.
I am mine.'

The Alphabet of Pain

Nobody has taught you or me
the alphabet of suffering.
Isn't it strange?
We attend so many schools
throughout life.
We learn so many different things,
and while most of them are useless,
nobody teaches us about
the most common thing
we experience in life.
Isn't it strange?
We enter adult life
as mature people,
yet entirely unqualified
to face suffering.
Nobody has taught you or me

how to cope with mourning,
loss,
grief,
loneliness,
or the sense of uselessness.
Nobody has taught you or me
how to scream
when the emotional pain becomes intense.
Nobody has taught you or me
what to say
when life gives us hard punches
and despair knocks us to the ground.
Nobody has taught you or me
how to ask for help,
the proper words to use,
and how to avoid clichés.
Nobody has taught you or me
how to be honest
with ourselves and others,
and never answer,
'I am fine, thank you.
I will call you soon.'
Nobody has taught you or me
how to hold our dignity
when we feel dead inside.

We enter adult life
as mature people,
yet we don't even know
how to trace the first letters
of the suffering alphabet.
We are so unprepared.
Isn't it strange to be emotionally illiterate
since pain is everywhere?
At least,
I hope
my poem is an alarm for you.
Wake up, friend.
Life is not a happy social media post.
Train your heart to be strong,
kind,
and humble.
This is how you can learn
the disruptive alphabet
of suffering,
and move on.

Reflections on Self-Love

When you wake up inside your soul,
you realize
that authentic self-love comes with
clarity,
self-respect,
self-awareness,
wisdom,
and compassion.
Make time for yourself.
Show more love to your beautiful soul.
Self-love will teach you
how to have healthy relationships.
You can't pour wisdom
from a broken or empty cup.

The Most Challenging Battle

Suffering is not a story
that always happens to someone else.
Suffering visits everybody,
including you.
It doesn't matter if you don't have time,
if you spend extra hours at work,
if you are kind or not,
if you are busy
doing nothing or doing great things.
Suffering will find you
anywhere you are
and whatever you do.
Suffering never makes appointments
or calls you in advance.
It just slams the door of your life
and enters.

'Here you are!'
Now,
what are you going to do?
Where can you hide?
Nowhere.
You have to face suffering.
It will not be easy.
It will be a cathartic moment
in your life.
You will never be the same.
Facing suffering is the beginning
of becoming a mature soul.
You will fight.
Cry.
Forgive.
Heal.
Let go.
Rise.
And in the end,
you will become strong.

Awakening to Maturity

Awakening to maturity is not easy.
It is a long process of gathering clarity,
empathy,
good judgment,
and wisdom.
One day,
you will realize
that you have not lived in vain.
You strived to do
something good and meaningful
with yourself.
Be grateful.
It is a privilege to wake up
to a deeper reality.
Some souls sleep their entire existence.

Time to Heal

Have you ever missed yourself?
Have you ever needed to talk
to your heart?
Have you ever felt
that you need time and space
only for yourself?
If so,
your time of awakening has come.
It is time to heal your soul.
Be present.
Don't be late
for the meeting with your beautiful soul.

Coming Home

Emotional healing is about coming home.
Slowly,
determinedly,
boldly.
Coming back to your heart
with a poem
in your mind.
One day,
I will be whole again.

Stop

You can break your own heart
blaming yourself
for past mistakes.
Stop this useless process.
Stop spending your adult life
recovering from your traumatic past.
Spend time rebuilding your inner self
and cleansing your soul.
It will help you live fiercely
from now on.

Speak Kindness

I don't remember the day
when I realized
that I know nothing
if my heart can't speak kindness.
But I remember the moment
when I looked into the mirror
and I made a promise:
'Every day,
I will try to become more fluent
in kindness.
Every day,
I will try to not hurt anyone.
Every day
I will remind myself
that unhealed souls are mean,
angry,

grumpy,
unhappy,
and insensitive.
Every day,
I will speak in kindness.
Every day,
I will try to become more fluent
in this beautiful language.'

Weaving Back Your Precious Self

Emotional healing is all about
weaving back your precious self.
You stitch your invisible wounds.
You sew your heart's cracks
with hope
and patience.
You stitch the gaps
between your past and present situation
with compassion.
You pray and heal.
You only crave a quiet life.

Healing Is a Sign

You never heal your heart's wounds
to get a badge of honor.
You heal yourself
to become stronger and wiser.
You heal yourself
to get the power to move on.
Healing is a sign of maturity.
A sign of self-respect.
A sign of dignity.
A sign of self-awakening.

An Ongoing Reminder

When you face an emotional collapse
and decide to heal yourself,
you become a loving parent
to your wounded heart.
And that is absorbing.
Every moment,
hold your inner child
in the arms of love
and patience.
One day,
you will figure out
how to fully heal your heart.
Until then,
stay busy being a loving parent
to your wounded self.

Not Your Responsibility

When you feel overwhelmed
with the chaos of this world,
remind yourself
that it is not your responsibility
to fix the madness of the world
or to carry
the heavy burden of this world
on your shoulders.
Don't whine about it.
Stop worrying about everything
that is going on out there.
You are not supposed
to become a collector
of disastrous news.
Turn your attention inward.
Watch what is going on

deep down
in your heart.
Remind yourself
that your only duty is
to heal yourself in peace.
This is how you can contribute
to a better world.
Start living in a place
of self-awareness,
quietness,
kindness,
love,
forgiveness,
and growth.
Start residing mainly in your heart
and less outside yourself.
You are the world that matters.

Go Inward

We spend our lives
running,
walking,
going back and forth,
yet everything essential happens
inside our souls.
Have you ever traveled inward?
Have you ever listened to your soul?
Have you talked
with your soul lately?
When was the last time
you had a dream?
When was the last time
you made a wish?
When was the last time
you wanted something for yourself?

When was the last time
you made a change to heal your life?
Go inward, my friend.
Spend your life
reconnecting with your true self.
Everything essential happens within.

Plant Undying Hopes

When you become self-aware,
you will have one thing to do
to live your life peacefully.
Plant undying hopes
in your heart.
Let them gestate,
gain roots,
evolve.
Pray.
One day,
you will admire beautiful flowers
springing up from your heart.

Twelve Things to Do for Healing

Be brave
and forgive.
Be wise
and look only inward.
Be kind
and validate your needs.
Be realistic
and remove the mountain
of your suffering
stone by stone,
feeling after feeling.
Be bold
and overcome your life barriers.
Be strong
and choose to heal
and save yourself.

Be good
and respect yourself.
Be humble
and look at everyone
with hope
in their healing.
Be persistent
and transform your vulnerable self.
Be free
and rise like a phoenix.
Be silent
and always bloom.
Be wild
and love again.

Healing Never Stops

Healing is a verb.
A dynamic verb.
Its action never stops,
for your change and growth never end.

Transform This Place

A broken heart is an unsafe,
inhospitable,
perilous place
where hidden demons can kill you.
You have only one choice.
Walk in,
tame those cruel demons,
and heal your wounds.
Turn your heart into a blissful place
where extraordinary things are possible.
Build a home for your soul
with all the hues and tints of hope.
Be calm and patient.
You need this transformative experience
to evolve and move on.

You Still Belong to Love

When someone breaks your heart,
remind yourself
that you still belong to love.

Your soul was made of love,
and is meant to love.
Don't let anything separate you
from the beauty of love.
Trust me;
I have been at this point in my life too,
and I realized something essential.
Sometimes,
bravery means embracing your wounds
and imperfections
through healing.
So, be brave, my friend.
It is time to heal your heart.
You are not destined
to live in grief,
loneliness,
or emotional brokenness.
Be brave
and heal yourself.
One day,
you will dare to love again.
Trust me;
I have been at this point in my life too.

You Will Heal

When life is hard on you,
find solace
in imagining something special:
What if I could be like a sunray?
Neither pain nor fear could catch you.
You would be wild and free.
You would spend your life in light,
peace,
and warmth.
Close your eyes
and promise to your beautiful soul,
'You will heal.
Neither pain nor fear will catch you.
You will heal.
You will be wild and free.'

Alexandra Vasiliu

Always Be Gentle

In all ways,
you should always try to be gentle.
Every heart has hidden wounds
that bleed.
Be gentle.

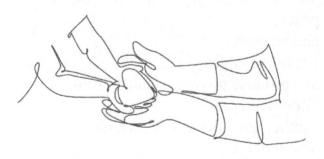

No broken heart can heal
without Band-Aids.
Be gentle.
Always be gentle.
Soft.
Meek.
Simple.
Be gentle.
Always be gentle.
You never know
what the person who sits next to you
has been through.
Be gentle –
this is proof you understood
your healing lessons.

Don't Waste Time

Don't waste time.
Don't spend the precious time
of your life
entertaining yourself
with childish things.
Take your life seriously,
learn how to do that,
gather wisdom.
Don't spend time collecting quotes;
that is not how maturity comes.
Don't swim
in the social media sea
and dream of mermaids.
You are a beautiful, unique soul,
with an amazing, unique story.

What You Need

Let the light enter your scarred heart
like a river flows
through rocks and cracks.
Let the light find a way
to touch your spirit,
heal,
and restore your precious self.
Above all else,
you are a ray of sunshine.

Two Options in Life

Sink or swim,
these are the only options in life.
It is up to you
which you choose.

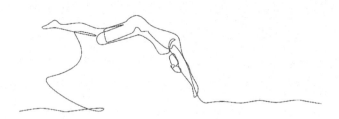

Through Your Heart

Be patient with yourself
when depression consumes you.
I know
that each day that passes
is a copy of the last.
I know
your heart has been swallowed
by darkness and grief.
I know
that you feel frozen within.
I know
you ask yourself,
What to do from now on?
Take heart.
Believe
that in time,

things will ease.
Be patient with yourself.
Emerging from darkness takes time.
Imitate a garden snail
that always carries its heavy house
and yet moves steadily forward.
Exit your depression.
There is beauty beyond the darkness.
Believe in that magical beauty.
Don't stop.
Move on.
Healing is all about moving on.

Ready to Learn

When you accept your suffering
with humility,
you are ready to learn
the meanings of life.

Wherever You Find

If you face adversities,
you know that
healing words,
love,
and prayers
can guard your heart.
My friend,
wherever you find
a healing word,
gather it into your heart,
for you found a rare gem.
Wherever love meets you,
open your heart and hug her,
for you found
the true physician
of your soul.

Wherever prayers cover you,
close your eyes,
and say *Thank you, God*,
for a door to hope and deep healing
has been opened for you.

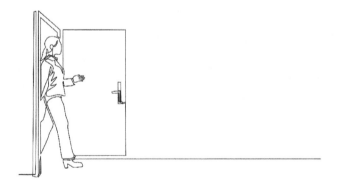

Within Your Heart

There is a transformative power
within your heart –
the power of self-love,
the power of hope,
the power of healing
and believing in yourself,
the power of starting all over again
and overcoming adversities,
the power of not giving up.
Bring to life
all these extraordinary abilities
that God gave you.
You are a beautiful soul.
Embrace your uniqueness.

Healing Comes in Peace

Your name is still scrawled
on the walls of my heart.
How can I ever cleanse them?
How can I ever learn
the art of letting go?
How can I ever forgive you
and move on?
How can I ever forget you?
Healing is a mystery to me.
Then, God whispered in my ear,
'Become silent in your heart,
stay still for a while,
and listen to the sounds
that flowers make
when they bloom.
Do you hear anything?

No.
Then, imitate those flowers.
Every perfect transformation is private
and silent.
Be quiet, my friend.
Stop the spin of questions,
and look inward.
Healing comes in peace.'

The Demons of Fear

Some people are afraid
to lose their material wealth.
They spend all their lives
fighting to protect it.

Like these people,
I have always been afraid
to lose my only wealth –
my inner peace,
my serenity.
I have spent thousands of days
learning how to protect my well-being.
But God taught me
that inner peace stays
as long as I cultivate healing,
love,
prayer,
forgiveness,
and resilience.

Dear Heart

Dear Heart,
I want to write a poem that soothes you,
but where can I find
those miraculous words?
I want to write a poem that heals you.
I want to write a poem that can save you.
I want to write a poem that tells you,
I love you for who you are.

Stay Here

If you are new to this healing journey,
then welcome.
Feel comfortable within yourself.
Don't be scared by all these unknowns.
Take it easy.
You will stay here
as long as you need.
Until then,
let me hug you
and tell you just,
'Welcome!
You are not alone, my dear.'

Build a Bridge

If you want to heal
your heart's wounds,
you will build a bridge
from the person you are today
to the person you want to become
in the foreseeable future.

Surround Yourself with Peace

Dear Heart,
start healing your wounds
and surround yourself with peace.
Every heart needs a fence of quietness.
You will need it
to learn to heal,
to forgive,
to trust
and love again.
Let my wisdom build this fence for you.

Start Healing Yourself

Stop carrying the weight
of your relationship trauma
wherever you go.

Turn your pain into prayer.
Turn your tears into wisdom.
Turn your depression into resilience.
Healing starts with self-awareness
and continues in peace.
Keep healing your wounds;
you do that for yourself
and for the one
who one day,
will want to live in your heart.
Keep healing your relationship anguish;
you do that for yourself
and for the one
who one day,
will find you
and love you dearly.
Keep healing your past;
you do that for yourself
and for the one
who one day,
will be your beautiful future.

Stand by Your Heart

If you are on a healing journey,
you should stand by your vulnerable self.
Don't leave your heart alone
to face pain,
demons,
and fears.
Stand by your heart
and fight face-to-face.
Sometimes,
fighting means having the courage to
heal.
Other times,
action means
saying *I love you* to your inner self.

A Sense of Belonging

Healing your emotional wounds
will give you a sense of belonging.
You will realize
that you belong to your beautiful soul.
And this is not a small thing,
for this forgotten sense will bring you
inner peace.

Do Something Beautiful

If you want to cure depression,
do something beautiful
for someone else.
Start with yourself.
Give a hug to your inner child.
Hold tight your scared self.
Say kind words to your soul.
Then, do something nice
for someone else.
Cook dinner
for someone you like.
Order a bouquet of tulips
for your neighbor.
Buy a few copies
of your favorite poetry book
and give them away to people

who might need them.
Buy ice cream
for all the kids
who live on your street.
Pray for each person you meet
in this life.
Do something beautiful and positive
every day
of your life.
Honor your soul
by building a decent life.
Fulfil your aspirations.
Make plans for your future.
Strive to create something extraordinary.
Your soul is sacred.
Don't let it drown in depression
and despair.
Exhume your soul from that darkness,
help it shine,
and do amazing things for yourself
and the others around you.

Into a Mine of Gold

Sit on the edge of your wounds,
yet don't be a passive watcher
of your emotions.
Pray to God
to transform each emotional injury
into a mine of gold.
You need to become a healing soul
in this cruel world.
Try to find yourself again
in everything you used to like and do.
Restore all your good habits.
When was the last time
you walked in the rain
without an umbrella?
When was the last time
you ran barefoot in the grass?

When was the last peaceful sunset
that you watched?
When was the last time
you studied a lovely painting?
When was the last time
you read a meaningful book?
When was the last time
you listened to a piece of beautiful music?
When was the last time
you laughed,
danced,
or daydreamed?
When was the last time
you planted a flower or a tree?
When was the last time
you watered your backyard?
When was the last time
you gazed at the stars?
When was the last time
you thought about your inner beauty?
When was the last time
you relished your own company?
Return to your precious self.
Heal your soul
and change your life for the better.

You Are Already Free

Nobody can ever incarcerate your heart.
As long as you dream,
you are free.
You are already free.

The Hard Way to Growth

Life is not a Hollywood movie.
Life is brutal.

You can't spare yourself from pain.
Instead of running away
from your problems,
from your emotional turmoil,
from your past
and your hidden traumas,
prepare yourself for this encounter.
Suffering is a way of life telling you,
'I am here to stay
until you become humble,
until you realize you are not special,
but a unique, normal human being
like everybody else.
I am here to teach you
to become self-conscious.
I will help you grow.'

Your Heart Is a Garden

Imagine your heart
as a beautiful garden.
Plant the flowers of love
in your heart.
Erase all toxic thoughts
as you would pull out weeds.
Pull out the weeds, my friend,
and keep your innocence.
Plant hope and self-forgiveness
in your mind.
Water the seeds of your heart
with boundless love.
Be resilient,
and transform your heart
into an amazing garden of serenity
and peace.

Make a Promise

In a world full of empty promises,
make a promise to yourself,
'My Dear Self,
I promise
I will love and respect you
beyond anyone else.'
This promise will protect you
against beggars
and thieves of innocence.

Stories to Tell

Each scar on your heart
has a story to tell.
Have you had time to read
all your secret narratives?
Have you had time to listen to
all your stories?
I know
you might feel scared,
yet you should gather the courage
to read
or listen to them.
Then, find time to heal your heart
and seed more love
deep in your scars.
Many of us are becoming too sour to love
and too bitter to believe in love.

Beauty Can Heal

Sometimes
suffering can make you feel numb
to inspiration and hope.
You feel dead inside.
Tired of yourself.
Tired of suffering.
Tired of everything.
Is there anything
in the world
that could touch your heart
in a positive way?
Get out of your shell,
take a walk in nature,
and restore your innocent curiosity,
your amazing sense of wonder.
When was the last time

you admired a butterfly,
a blossoming wildflower,
a blue jay,
a fern,
a sunset?
Walk in nature,
savor the slowness of the day,
and forget your heavy feelings for a
while.
Nurture your heart
with peace and simplicity,
and remind yourself that
beauty can heal.

A Little Prayer

Before you get out of bed
every morning,
say a little prayer,
'Dear God,
please help me heal
so everything inside me
will speak about love and kindness.
Make my heart a book about You,
a poem of compassion.
Dear God,
help me appreciate
all the beautiful souls
I will be meeting today.'
Start every new day
with this healing approach.
Build positive habits,

so you can appreciate this life
that has been given to you
by our Creator.
Each life needs to be healed,
so does yours.
Be grateful.
Stay in the light.
This is what you need the most.

Only Forward

Your soul starts to grow
when you realize
that healing is a one-way trip –
only forward.

The Goals of Healing

When you heal your wounded heart,
you do it for yourself
and for those
who one day,
will need your whole heart,
will yearn for a home,
a place of love and harmony.
Strive to heal, my friend.
You do it for yourself
and for those
who one day,
will love you
and will need to be loved
with your whole, beautiful heart.

A Permanent Reminder

If you heal your broken heart,
bring your bright experience
into the world.
Tell healing stories
to the broken ones.
Speak about your healing process.
Speak fearlessly.
Say out loud,
'We were created with love.
That is the actual DNA
of our personalities.
And love can heal.
Be brave, my friends.
Dare to love.
Dare to heal.
Healing is all about love.

Healing is a permanent reminder
of how to love ourselves
and those around us.
Be brave.
Your story is not over yet.'

A Way of Life

Becoming a flourishing soul
should never be your ultimate goal.
It should be your way of life.
Heal, rise, and bloom –
these are the directions of your life.
That is what self-love should ignite
in you
and in all of us.

Something Special

If your kindness percolates into
others' hearts,
then you master
something quite special –
the most beautiful non-verbal way
in which
you can say,
'My heart has been healed.'

One More Wish

Forget your problems for a few moments.
Make a wish.
Then, make a new wish.
Don't break the spell.
Allow yourself to be a child again.
Make another wish
and another one
until you go to bed.
In the end,
your inner pockets will be full of dreams.
Is there anything wrong
with behaving like a child
and aiming to escape depression,
even if it is just for a day?

Not a Disparate Chapter

Don't let your healing experience become
a disparate chapter
in your book's life.
Make your healing experience
a daily habit.
Allow this mindset to nurture
your inner transformation.
You are the only one
who can turn a new page
and rewrite the chapters
of your life.
Strive to embrace change.
Start writing the first chapter
of your new story,
'I will heal.'
Let your healing experience be

the silver lining,
and keep writing
beautiful new chapters
of growth
and personal transformation.

Find Someone

Find someone
who can admire the entire ocean
in one drop,
and see your wonderful heart
in one word –
and that word would be *emotion*.
Find someone
who can sail the seas of life
bravely,
and protect your heart
fearlessly –
and that courage would mean *love*.
Find someone
who can contemplate the world daily
and cherish you timelessly –
and that joy would be *forever*.

Choose

Choose those people
who help your heart rise again
like a bright sun.
They will love you
without hurting you.
Love comes through
a fresh stream of trust.

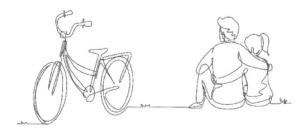

There Will Come a Day

One day,
you will rise again,
soaring from the abyss
of your inner chaos.
The ice
that froze your heart
will melt,
making room for light
and hope.
One day,
you will rise again.

The Cemetery of Your Past

When there is no one around
to watch you
visiting the cemetery of your past,
light a candle
to the tomb of your old self,
and say,
'I came here to tell you
that I didn't forget you,
and I guess
I will never forget you.
Life is not about burying
the imperfect images of myself.
I will always keep you in my mind
as a reminder
to never act again
like I did.

I came here to tell you
that life is about accepting my faults,
fixing them,
and rising again
much wiser than before.
I came here
to tell you
I will never forget you,
But I will not live
like a victim.
I will heal myself
with love and self-acceptance.
I will empower myself
with self-confidence,
faith,
and hope.
One day,
I will shine again.
One day,
I will become the wonderful person
I was created to be.'
Then,
leave that place
and let the candlelight
into the cemetery of your past.

Not Alone Anymore

When you face life challenges,
find comfort in my words.
Look upward to the sky
for a few moments
and say,
'From this day on,
I will replace the pronoun *I*
with the expression *God and I.*
I will start walking
on my life's road
with God.
If I limp,
God will support me,
so *God and I* will keep walking.
If I stumble,
God will help me rise,

so *God and I* will keep moving forward.
If I can't find a solution
to my life's problems,
God will illuminate my mind,
so *God and I* will find a pathway.
I will no longer be alone.
From this day on,
God and I will work together
to become friends.'

You Are a Gift

Be gentle with yourself.
You are a gift.
You are a precious gift
for yourself
and the world.
Be gentle with yourself
and don't break the perfect gift
that is hidden
deep down in your heart.

An Open Door

If someone dismantles your life,
be the first
to gather
the shattered pieces of your broken heart.

That catastrophic event can be
a catalyst
for you.
Don't spend your days crying
and sobbing.
Don't let your trauma shape
your life.
It is the perfect time to heal yourself.
Start your healing journey today.
There is an open door
within your heart.
Enter through that secret door
and embrace your vulnerable self.
You need love,
so show much love
to your inner child.
Hug your soul
and make a promise:
'I have the power to choose.
And I choose to heal my wounds.
I choose to repair my shattered life
with love,
kindness,
faith,
and acceptance.

'I choose to fight for my life,
change myself,
and accomplish my full potential.
I choose to find the determination
to move forward.
I want to live beautifully.'
Spend time with your precious self,
heal your every wound,
and empower your soul
with love,
kindness,
faith,
and acceptance.
One day,
you will contemplate
your remarkable metamorphosis.

Unavoidable

Where are you going?
You can't run away from suffering.

There is no place
where you can get immunity
from pain.
Suffering is unavoidable
and ubiquitous.
Wherever you go,
it will find you.
Don't aim to become
a *hippie* at heart.
It is not realistic.
Better you gather courage,
wisdom,
clarity,
strength,
and inner peace.
You need all these virtues
to protect your soul
when suffering attacks you.

Your Home

Healing is your true home.
Stay here as long as you need warmth,
love,
peace,
and acceptance.
Stay.
Healing is a blessed home.

Avoid Self-Sabotage

If you are in a damaged relationship,
stop being in denial.

Avoid self-sabotage,
and accept the truth –
this relationship hasn't worked out.
Let go of anyone
who stops you from evolving
through love.
Take yourself out of this relationship
that is no longer aligned with
your emotional needs.
Return to yourself.
Pray more.
Start healing
your hidden emotional wounds.
One day,
you will be ready to fly again
like a brave eagle.

You Are Not Supposed

When you want to change your life,
you are not supposed
to visualize your future in detail.
You already know
you want peace and love.
That should be enough
to articulate your thoughts
and take action toward change.
Set goals
and act in such a way
that you will achieve them.
Every day,
focus on healing your wounded self
and building a new life.
Practice self-witnessing.
Keep praying to God.

Keep a diary
and write down your feelings.
Say 'I love you,'
and 'I am sorry'
to your soul
more consistently.
Be kind to yourself
and encourage others
to show their compassion more often.
Change your emotional
and cognitive behavior
and take deliberate steps toward
positivity.
With this understanding,
one day,
your goals will become a reality
and you will reach the desired outcomes.

Be the First

If your repressed emotions explode
one day,
be the first
who will hug your inner child.
Be the first
who will treat your soul
with kindness
and understanding.
Don't spend time creating stories
about your anger
or failure.
Be the first
who will realize
that you need love and healing
to be emotionally healthy again.

Is There Anyone?

Is there anyone
in this world
who could touch my heart
with the gentle hands of love?
I wish
there could be someone
who believes that
healing is all about love.
And together,
we could heal our hearts.

To Move Forward

Find a caring soul
who is honest
and supportive of you.
Find a beautiful soul
who helps you rise from ashes.
Find a loving soul
who always saves
a few healing words
only for you.
It is all you need
to dare to move forward.

Educate Yourself

Never let betrayals hinder your growth.
Never let sadness pull you down
to the hell of harming yourself.
Never let tears drown your soul.
Never let negativity control your
thoughts.
All these are deadly toxins
that slowly poison
and kill your heart.
No matter how many adversities
you have been through,
educate yourself
to become emotionally stable
and mentally strong.
Even if you do it through gritted teeth,
just educate yourself to become mature.

Life is a wrestling match.
There will be moments
when you are thrown to the ground,
and your mouth tastes the dust.
Brace yourself
to confront difficulties.
Life is not a filtered image
from social media.
Stay strong.
Train yourself to deal
with disappointment,
and don't underestimate
your determination
that will help you overcome
many tough circumstances.
Gather wisdom and inner strength
for the challenging moments
of your life.
Find realistic solutions
to your problems.
Make good use of all the gifts
that God planted in your heart.
Pray every day.
Practice mindfulness and kindness
whenever you can.

Honor God
and show love to your soul
by choosing to live
faithfully and intentionally.
One day,
you will be surprised
to see how far you can fly.

Fight for Your Precious Self

Depression has an incredible power
to dehumanize a person.
You feel caught in darkness
like an eagle in a trap.
You are stuck,
although you want to fly.
Depression makes you feel invisible
and insignificant.
My dear friend,
these feelings are not permanent,
and they can't define you.
Look at yourself in the mirror
and say to your inner child:
'I will heal from depression.
I will set myself free.
I will let my inner beauty prevail.

I will believe in my great potential.
I will embrace my heart every day,
and fight for my future.
I will heal.
I am a beautiful soul
praying for a second chance.
All I want is to have the opportunity
to show my inner beauty,
to love again,
to forgive,
to help others,
and to contribute
to the good of humanity.
I want to grow with light
and live meaningfully.
I am a beautiful soul
praying to break free.
I will heal.
I will fight for my healing.
I want to come back to life
and rise
like a bold phoenix.
I will heal.
I owe it to myself.'

How to Make Good Choices

You don't need pills
to gather the courage
to let go of toxic relationships.
You don't need pills
to gain clarity of mind.
You don't need pills
to affirm what is wrong with you.
You don't need pills
to learn to make peace
with your vulnerable self.
You don't need pills
to learn how to love your precious self.
You don't need pills
to fight for your aspirations.
You don't need pills
to help you make good choices in life.

You don't need pills
to become smart and wise.
You don't need pills
to remind yourself
that peace and harmony are the antidotes
to your chaotic life.
You don't need pills
to pray every day
and find the pure way to God.
You don't need pills
to live beautifully
with a humble spirit.
All you need to do
is return to the core of simplicity –
ask God where that path is,
and follow it.
Pray for the rest of your life.
Tie your soul to the beauty of heaven,
and you will enter a world of peace,
healing, knowledge, and love.
You will envelop yourself
with gratitude and hope.
You don't need pills
to get to live that day.

Stay Kind

One way of rising above adversity
is to stay kind
despite everything
that you have been through.
Don't let your suffering control you.
Don't let your past make you
bitter and hostile.
Be kind.
Always be kind.
No matter how many obstacles
you encounter in life,
spread love
and compassion.
Always have a kind word
on your lips.
Always keep a smile

in your heart
for whomever you may meet.
Stay kind.
That is the key
to overcoming adversities.

Use That Fuel

If your emotional life is a failure,
don't blame anyone for that mess.
Do the best you can
to use the disappointment
as a fuel
to discover your unique self.
Examine your soul.
Do you genuinely love yourself?
You can't love anyone
if you don't respect and love yourself
first.
Start a journey of self-discovery.
Avoid betraying your conscience.
Avoid bad habits
that numb your frustrations.
Avoid living trapped

in a downward spiral.
Face your emotional reality.
The moment you accept the truth,
you open the doors to your heart.
You will learn to love your unique soul.
You will find a pathway to healing
and acquiring wisdom.
You will become aware
of your inner imperfections,
and work on them.
You will rebuild your life
on solid foundations.
One day,
you will embrace your soul
with hope and self-acceptance.
One day,
you will realize
that self-love is a strength
that helped you move on.
One day,
you will sit in silence and gratitude
for this journey of self-discovery.
Your life will never be a mess again.

On Little Cat Feet

Sometimes
hope comes on little cat feet.
Never mind.
Open your heart
and allow hope to illuminate you.
Peace will cover you
slowly and steadily.

Not in One Day

You can't heal your trauma
in one day.
Be patient.
Healing is a reconstruction process
that takes time and energy.
You will plant beauty in each scar
of your soul.
You will sprinkle hope
in each wound of your heart.
You will nourish your past
with self-acceptance
and clarity.
Be patient.
Rebuilding your soul is one
of the most important duties
that you have in your lifetime.

Don't Be Afraid

Don't be afraid
that you are not a professional healer.
Fear causes underestimation
of your inner powers.
Have you ever thought
that you are brave and strong?
God created you
with magnificent powers.
Use them to mend your soul.
Just look at yourself
through the lens of love.
You are a brave wounded eagle
looking for healing and kindness.
But one day,
you will be ready to soar again.
The beautiful blue sky will embrace you.

The Real Beauty of Existence

You are never done with your healing.
It is a daily process
for the rest of your life.
But this is the real beauty of existence –
to do the work on yourself,
to grow,
and let your most authentic self flourish
day after day,
year after year.

Like the Woods

The woods sleep and rest
in the wintry weather.
Follow their example
and go inside your heart.
Find inner peace.
Take a rest there.
Daydream.
One day,
spring will embrace you.
One day,
hope will make your heart bloom again.
One day,
you will come back to life
like the woods
after the wintry weather.

Unavailable for Despair

As long as your heart shelters dreams
worth living,
you can escape from despair.
Rise from your ashes,
get up from your sadness,
and give birth to your aspirations,
you are a *mother-to-be*.
Don't be afraid,
you have so much to work on,
you have so many dreams
to bring to life.
Fight for them.
Fight for your aspirations.
You can always be a loving parent
to your wounded heart.

Be Spiritually Awake

If you are spiritually awakened,
you are present in your heart.
From this moment on,
you will open yourself
to the miracles of healing.

Pray

If your mind orbits around dark thoughts,
change their trajectory.
Place your thoughts
in the middle of prayers.
'Oh, Lord,
help me build a life
of light and hope.
Arrange my life
as only You can do.
Please cast away the demons
of fear and depression
that disrupt my life.
Help me heal
and find peace again.'

Smile Back

Even if you go
through many challenges,
keep healing your wounds.
Persevere with working on yourself.
Uproot yourself from toxic things,
spread a sense of generosity
in everything you do,
smile often,
forgive yourself and others,
and love more.
One day,
life will smile back at you.

Be Kind

Know that the human condition
has always been linked to pain.
You are not an exception.
You will never be able
to avoid pain.
You will hurt others,
and others will hurt you.
You will be disappointed by others,
and others will disappoint you.
You will leave others,
and others will leave you.
What you can avoid is
to hurt and disappoint someone
on purpose.
Be kind.
Stay kind.

Always keep in mind
that every heart has
thousands of wounds
that are not fully healed.
Be kind.
Every heart has passed
through wars
that were not won.
Stay kind.
Stay compassionate.
Educate yourself
to have a greater sense of empathy
and understanding.
In this brutal,
hectic world,
there is always a shortage
of kind people.
Be wise,
meek,
and caring.
Learn to navigate
through the challenging moments
of life.
Every soul faces the same struggles.
Never forget

that being mean is easy,
vulgar,
and self-destructive,
and being kind
and loving
is the only challenge
that will help you evolve.
Be kind, my friend.
And continue your healing journey.

Still Healing

You are still healing yourself
if you constantly reflect upon
your flaws and imperfections,
and upon everything
that keeps you stuck in your past.
You are still healing.
And that is wonderful progress.

The Unchanged Season

The seasons change regularly,
yet it would be best
if you choose to stay
in the uninterrupted season of love.
Be loyal to your heart
and live in that particular season.
The beauty of love will lead you
toward more peace,
healing,
and harmony.
Your inner gifts will never wither.

Still Working on Yourself

If someone asks you,
'How are you doing?'
answer honestly,
'Still healing.'
That is the naked truth.
Throughout life
you gathered vulnerabilities,
tears,
fears,
insecurities,
pains,
failures,
bruises,
and disappointments.
How could you not choose
to heal yourself?

Whoever you are,
face the truth, my friend.
You are still healing.
You are still working on yourself.
And that is the bravest thing
you can do
in this damaged, sick world.

No Control

Whoever you are
who reads these lines,
make a promise to your soul,
'It is time to heal my inner child.
It is time to rebuild myself.
It is time to move on.'
Whoever you are
who reads these lines,
don't be afraid.
Believe in the power
of your metamorphosis.
Your past can't have control over you
as long as you decide to change
and strive to heal.

Don't Prove

Never try to prove to others
how kind, forgiving, or loving
you truly are.
Don't live
as if you perform on a stage.
Show your soul to God.
Let Him know
how kind, forgiving, and loving
you truly are.
Live peacefully,
and be aware
that you live within God's hands.

I Will Help You Rise

Find someone
who can love you deeply
and promises you,
'I will help you rise,
and you will never be the same.'

Time to Change Yourself

It is always time to be kind.
Kindness never goes out of style.
Be kind to yourself,
and you will look beautiful.
Be kind to others,
and you will shine.

The Invisible World

There is more to life than you see.
There are feelings,
emotions,
dreams,
aspirations –
an entire world of love and wonders.
Work on your invisible world
and make it visible to others.
Help everyone see their soul.
Help them contemplate
their beautiful unseen.
That is what healing is all about.

Parenting Your Soul

Look at you –
you are a grown-up,
with a child
in your arms –
your soul.
What will you do with this child
from now on?
Will you make time
to educate your inner child?
Will you nurture your inner little one
with love,
great virtues,
patience,
and important values?
Will you embrace your soul
whenever you are asked?

Will you encourage your sweet child
whenever needed?
Will you fight to give
a promising future
to your precious child?
What will you do with this child
from now on?
Ask yourself.
Don't come up with a superficial answer.
Whoever you are,
please reflect on my poem.
You have been through many situations,
you know so many things.
You are a grown-up now.
But look at you –
you are no longer alone.
You carry a child
in your arms –
your soul.
Look inward –
your soul is helpless,
vulnerable,
totally dependent on you,
on your mind,
on your choices.

Your soul is not the same age as you.
Your soul is a young child.
Now, you have a responsibility –
to help your soul grow,
thrive with love,
and embrace life with hope.
Dedicate your time
to raise your inner child.
Devote yourself to helping your soul
become mature.
Be wise and patient.
Raising a child takes time and energy.
Consider parenting your soul
as a way of learning
how to heal yourself.
Cherish that particular time
and do it with dignity.
In the end,
the reward will be your peace.
And reaching inner peace is one
of the most outstanding achievements
in life.

No Emotional Manipulation

Don't let anyone mistreat you
or emotionally manipulate you.
Set boundaries.
Don't hold resentments.
Grow with wisdom,
inner strength,
and clarity.
Be self-aware –
some people will always try
to pull you into their toxicity.

Resist

Healing is a form of resistance.
You don't give up hope.
You don't throw in the towel.
You don't despair.
You don't capitulate.
You are still fighting for yourself.
You are struggling
to overcome your past.
You are healing
your invisible wounds.
What great proof of bravery!

Feel Safe

In a time of loss and loneliness,
remind yourself
that healing is not a temporary refuge.
Healing is your welcoming home
where you feel safe,
loved,
protected,
and empowered.

Don't Be a Drifter

Don't be a drifter.
Trees don't move roots
from place to place,
and nor do you.
Grow out of your soul.
Grow with love and resilience.
Stay strong in your evolution.
Day by day,
you will blossom into a charming person.

Seriously

Take your healing experience seriously.
Work hard on your heart.
Don't aim for superficial improvements.
Assume your transformation.
Address your fundamental problems,
so one day,
you will see yourself changed,
healed,
and with a new, beautiful mindset.
Take your healing experience seriously,
so one day,
you will realize
there is no shortage of compassion
in your heart.

The Most Significant Triumph

Devote yourself
to the process of healing.
There is no greater reward
for a broken heart.
It doesn't matter
if you win or not.
What is essential right now is not
the fame of a champion,
but rather the labor of striving
toward hope.
Keep fighting
with determination.
If you are not fighting,
you will regress
toward more pain,
so don't give up.

One day,
you will appreciate
your indomitable spirit,
and that will be
the most significant triumph
over your past.

A Different Alchemy

Suffering can be a chapter in your life
or your whole life book.
What you can do is include suffering
in your healing story.
Transform your hurt into hope.
Alchemy is not only about gold.
It is about your soul
that needs metamorphosis.

No Shame

If you are still healing,
there is nothing to be ashamed of.
You accepted the truth
that healing is not a speed test,
but rather a process of being present
in your heart
for the rest of your life.
Be grateful for acquiring this knowledge.
Keep healing your heart,
stay meek and humble,
awake and uncomplicated
in all the years that come.

Ask for Help

If you fall inside your dark thoughts
and it seems you never reach an end,
pray.
Praying is the healing connection
with God.
He is such a patient listener.
His light will give you wings
to fly over
the desert of depression.
Tell God more about your soul
and your unmet emotional needs.
Tell God about your turmoil.
Ask for illumination and inner peace.
Ask God to cut your toxic ties
with depression.
Ask God for protection,

guidance,
healing,
and help.
Ask God to bring you back
to life
and offer you meaningful healing.
Ask for a change.
Divine intervention can model your life
in a beautiful way.
Pray.
Only prayer will bring you hope.

The Second Nature

When you heal,
don't look back on your past.
A butterfly never misses its cocoon days.
Strive to heal
until you feel
that kindness is your second nature.
On that day,
you will realize that it is a great habit
to be kind to your soul
and others' souls too.
Practicing kindness is a subtle way
of admitting
I am healed.
Kindness is a sign of healing.
A sign that you are forever changed
in a beautiful way.

Spread your wings now,
and dare to fly.
Whoever you are,
be thankful
that you didn't choose to live
as if you were subhuman.
You decided to overcome your past
and never look like those who hurt you.
You chose to heal.
Whoever you are,
be grateful for your achievement.
Kindness is more than proof of humanity,
it is a sign of a noble soul,
and so are you.

Do Something Noble

Unplug yourself
from the social nonsense
and heal your wounded soul.
Don't numb your conscience
with false joys
and artificial goals.
Don't spend your time stuck
in the shallows of life.
Strive to rise from ashes,
to overcome obstacles,
to heal,
to build a beautiful identity,
and have a decent life.
Strive to do something noble
with yourself.
That is the best way

to become whole again
and be helpful to others.
Rise.
Rise from ashes.

A Great Mindset

Let go of painful memories.
Stop being haunted by ghosts
and the shadows of your past.
Hurt can't define you.
It is time to heal your heart
and move forward.
That is a great mindset to have.
Sometimes,
healing is all about letting go
and forgiveness.
Sometimes,
that is the recipe for survival.

Overcoming Depression

When you want to overcome depression,
do one thing.
Stop playing the same song
on a continuous loop
in your head,
'I am not good.
I am not worthy of love.'
Stop underestimating your beautiful soul.
Stop creating stories
that validate your insecurities.
Break the chain of your false beliefs.
Never let depression ruin you.
Dare to heal your wounded heart.
Dare to heal your vulnerable mind.
Dare to embrace yourself
and appreciate your unique worth.

Exit your comfort zone.
Transform your healing into
a creative recovery.
Use your imagination.
Take a walk in the woods,
collect colorful leaves,
and admire God's world.
Connect your heart
to the beauty of nature.
Use a diary
and write down your feelings
and thoughts.
Paint a picture
with vibrant or pastel colors.
Seed flowers.
Decorate your room
with stunning artwork.
Nurture your heart
with something positive and uplifting.
Ponder over the best in your life.
Find peace in simplicity.
Pray to God daily.
His help will tutor you
on what to do
to find peace and solace.

Keep fighting for yourself.
Much hope is ahead waiting for you.
One day,
you will realize
that your healing has been
a complex journey
of finding self-esteem,
peace,
and inner strength.

Lean on Good Friends

In a time of healing,
don't waste your energy
with people
who don't value your potential
and let you wallow in self-pity.
Don't unfurl the petals
of your delicate self
toward those with hostile hearts.
Lean on good friends.

You need their kindness and inclusiveness
to alleviate your suffering.
You need their practical wisdom
to grow in spirit.
You need their hugs, love, and care
to heal completely.
If you don't have friends,
search for God.
He has everything
that you have ever needed.
His magnificent help will restore
your life.
Embrace this spiritual path.
It is time to heal
your lonely, scarred heart.

An Identity Journey

When life doesn't go
the way you imagined it would,
remind yourself that
it is time to heal.
Heal your existence.
Heal your soul.
Heal your heart and feelings.
Heal your mind and thoughts.
Heal your desires.
Heal everything
that you have known about yourself.
Somewhere,
along the way,
you will understand
that you can change
in a meaningful way.

On that day,
I hope you will remember my words:
Healing is an identity journey.

Be a Sunflower

Compare your life to a sunflower.
Have you always revolved around light?
Have you always looked to the bright side
of life?
Have you consistently grown with love?
Have you always spread
your rays of love,
gratitude,
and joy?
Have you always searched for freedom
and enlightenment?
Have you always flourished
in a season of warmth
and harmony?
If you find yourself
in the wrong place,

strive to grow roots
in a peaceful place.
Settle there
and change your life for the better.
Put aside fears,
competition,
and social barriers.
Look inward
where you can find meaning.
Dive into a tranquil lake of peace.
Dive deeper every day.
You can heal your past wounds.
Forget about the dangerous fields
of life.
Focus on your soul.
Discover your beautiful uniqueness.
Appreciate the calmness
and the serenity
that surround you.
What else can you wish for
when you have everything that matters?
Remind yourself that
your soul is a vibrant,
golden,
wild sunflower,

turning its pure face to peace.
Cultivate peace,
bloom quietly
with grace,
spread softly light
and joy,
and you will always stand out
like a precious sunflower.

Be Different

When you face difficult moments
trying to heal your trauma,
remind yourself,
'Never become
like those who hurt you.'
Don't judge those who harmed you.
Don't hold grudges and bitterness.
Don't make plans for revenge.
You have something greater
in your heart –
you have kindness,
you have the inner power
to forgive those unhappy souls,
you have the strength to overcome
that painful life experience.
Be kind to you.

Be understanding with your soul.
Make a commitment
to forgive yourself
and to forgive those who hurt you.
Forgiveness is the most powerful form
of freedom.
Forgiveness will set you free.
Be free, my friend.
Release your soul from
every traumatic prison
you have ever known.
You deserve to make peace
with your past.
You deserve to live in harmony
with your soul.
You deserve to overcome your trauma.
Remind yourself
that those who hurt you
don't have the power
to leave an indelible mark on you.
Remind yourself
that you can always heal.
Consistent healing can rewrite the ending
of your story
and ignite your hopes.

One day,
you will believe in yourself again.
One day,
you will be able to start over
and build a beautiful life.
One day,
your soul will be strong and wise.
Now,
the time
to heal from your trauma has come.
It is your time.
Embrace it.
Start your emotional healing journey
with kindness,
compassion,
and forgiveness.
These are precious gifts
that you give to yourself
to heal your soul.
These are great choices
that you make
to heal your soul.
Be kind.
Be compassionate.
Forgive.

Be free.
Move toward wholeness.
You have the power
to change your soul,
not those who hurt you.
Plant this thought in your wounds.
That is how you will build self-esteem
during your healing journey.
That is how you will make
your healing journey smoother.
That is how
those who hurt you
can never leave an indelible mark
on your soul.
Remind yourself,
I will heal.
I will heal.
And that will be your power.

For Hope

Healing is personal advocacy for hope.
While you mend your emotional wounds,
you mitigate against despair.
You hold onto hope
and that is the simplest way
to wish yourself the best.
One day,
while you are still healing,
you will notice
that your glimmer of hope has become
a torch of faith and strength.

A Deep Healing Connection

Whenever you hug a broken heart,
you will notice
that love is not a sensation,
yet a deep healing connection.
Hug a broken heart,
talk with that person,
listen to the person's story,
go an extra mile and pray for their soul.

The Permanent Self-Awakening

Emotional healing is not a journey
from point A to point Z,
nor a destination.
Healing is a transition
toward permanent self-awakening.
Open up your heart
to that profound wisdom.
You will be forever changed.

Healing Is a Country

Healing is a country
where on the first visit,
you may feel like a foreigner.
Everything is new and unfamiliar.
You don't know what to do,
how to speak,
how to behave.
You know nothing.
How can you feel welcome?
Where to go?
Where to settle?
How can you adjust?
Don't give up.
It is so easy
to go back to
where you came from.

It takes a lot of courage
to live in this country.
Even though
you might feel uncomfortable,
take comfort in knowing
that you are not alone.
Healing is the country
for all those who want to break free.

We are all called to live here.
Some of us are commuters –
we go back and forth
daily or even hourly.
We go back to the past
and then, go forward toward healing.
Other people are pilgrims –
they visit this land,
work on their hearts a little,
and then,
return to their countries of origin.
Don't judge them;
healing is not an easy practice.
Take comfort in knowing
that most of us settled here,
and we are here to stay.
Healing is our country
where we live in alignment
with our innate needs and aspirations.
Come here.
Feel welcome.
Healing is the only country
where you can grow and thrive.

Spark Your Imagination

Imagine
that your life
could be described in one word.
What would it be?
Love?
Healing?
Forgiveness?
Overcoming?
Devotion?
Imagine
that one word could heal your heart.
What would it be?
Forgiveness?
Acceptance?
Joy?
Kindness?

Love?
Imagine
that one word could change your heart.
What would it be?
Love?
Forgiveness?
Devotion?
Clarity?
Bravery?
Keep these uplifting words in your heart.
Embrace them
like you would hug your kids.
In this world of hate,
these special words might
become threatened
with extinction.

Demolish That Prison

Depression is a prison.
You can choose to be its inmate
for many months ahead
or you can choose
to live free.
Demolish that prison
brick by brick,
thought by thought.
Change your mindset.
Heal your thoughts,
heal your words,
revitalize your self-esteem,
and you will escape that prison.

Healing from Cruel Words

The way a cruel word
penetrates your heart
is the same way
the light enters
your underlying wounds.
Erase that harsh word
from your heart and mind
as you would remove a bullet
from your body.
Use the gentle hands of love,
clean your emotional injury
with forgiveness,
and cover the bleeding wound
with hope.
Be patient.
Healing may take longer,

for you suffer for two persons:
yourself
and the person who hurt you.
There will come a day
when you become aware
that the victim has not been you,
but the person who hurt you.
On that day,
let light teach you
how to let go of
all the dark, painful, cruel words.
Light will tutor you in mastering peace.

Find Strength

Find strength in this simple truth:
those who hurt you
teach you
how not to behave.
You don't want to copy that behavior.
You don't want to be harsh.
You don't want to hurt
other people's feelings.
You don't want to harm anyone.
Now, you have a realistic alternative.
Make a wise choice
and act decisively.
Allow yourself to be meek and humble.
Be kind
and become kinder
with every new day.

Make a difference in people's lives.
Teach them with your life
that kindness is everything
that anyone will ever remember.
Teach them
to change themselves
in such a way
that kindness will always be
their invisible business cards.
Be kind, my friend.
Your most authentic self will shine.
Be kind
and life will give you many opportunities
to praise its beauty.
Be kind.
There is no greater comfort
in this unforgiving world.
Be kind
and find strength, my friend,
in being kinder and kinder
with every new day.
Be kind –
that is a blessing.

A Reflection of Kindness

When your time for healing comes,
you will look at the world
with wise eyes.
You will notice
how easily people harm others.
They use cruel words
and evil-looking eyes
like irresponsible people use rifles
and crazily shoot bullets.
You will see
how unremorsefully people kill your soul.
The more you see,
the more you understand
that you are given a choice.
You can be like others
and use your invisible gun

whenever you dislike someone
or something.
Or, you can choose
to become different
and follow the challenging path
of self-healing.
Despite everything
that happens around you,
you can choose to become
a reflection of love,
goodness,
and kindness.
Choose to become a noble soul.
Life is too short
to live cynically,
corruptly,
promiscuously.

Renew Your Life

You will find the path to self-respect
when you are on your healing journey.
Keep this brief reminder
in your heart
and strive to renew your life.

Give Birth to Your Dreams

As long as your heart shelters dreams
worth living,
you can escape depression.
Give birth to your aspirations and goals.
Be bold;
you are the parent-to-be
of your future.

Start Looking Inward

If you go through trials,
and feel down,
crushed into millions of pieces,
don't expect unicorns and dragons
to save you.
Be a changemaker,
overturn that unsafe situation,
and start healing your life.
Fight hard.
Do the best you can
to find light and peace.
Start looking inward.
Sometimes,
the future is a quiet whisper
hidden in your heart.

Find That Bridge

If you ever wander aimlessly
through the ruins
of your dreams,
take a second look around you.
Somewhere nearby,
there is a bridge
that spans the gap
between your inner chaos
and your hopes.
Be bold
and cross that bridge.
Don't look back.
Don't look forward.
Keep traversing that bridge.
That is how your healing will start.
And before you reach

the other side of the bridge,
you will discover
an abundance of new dreams
in your young heart.

Healing Is All About Love

Healing is all about love –
love toward God
who created you for joy and meaning;
love toward your precious self;
love toward your loved ones
who wish you all the best.
Healing is all about hope –
you will overcome everything
that holds you back;
you will rise again,
and your future will offer you
beautiful surprises.
Healing means experiencing wonders.

Like a Sieve

If there are so many holes
in your soul
that it looks like a sieve,
don't fall into despair.
Look up to the sky.
Each hole is a window.
Emotional brokenness is an invitation
to talk directly with God.
Look up to the sky,
unlock your feelings,
and allow yourself to be healed
through divine love and grace.

A Heart-Shaped Stone

When you find a heart-shaped stone
at the beach,
please pick it up.
That unique stone is perfect –
no cracks,
no scars,
no holes,
no streams of tears.
Look at it carefully.
It is a *heart*
that never feels anything.
My friend,
don't pay that price
to never suffer again.
Don't become petrified.
Keep your heart alive.

Keep your heart fallible,
your heart is imperfectly beautiful
and imperfectly brave.
Full of scars,
full of wounds,
and dried tears,
your heart is proof
of being alive,
free,
fragile,
wild,
sensitive,
and bold.
Your heart is not a perfect stone,
yet a haven
for both your glorious
and uncomfortable feelings.

Layer After Layer

Peel the layers of pain
from your heart.
Heal your beautiful self.
Don't rush.
Take off layer after layer
until you get to the essence
of your heart.
Who are you deep inside?
What do you see
in your deepest depths?
What do you want to become?
What life do you want to have?
Reflect on essential questions,
aim for change,
and keep healing your precious self.

Quiet, Please!

There is so much advice
in the world
that you can no longer hear
your heart's needs.
Quiet the world's loud voice.
Sit with your thoughts in peace.
Get to know what you truly want.
Dive into a meaningful quietness.
Sometimes,
silence heals.
Sometimes,
silence speaks the healing words
that you need the most.
Sometimes,
silence brings you more clarity.
What path should you choose

in life
from now on?
Keep your mind open.
Remain silent,
calm,
mindful,
patient,
pure,
and above all,
grateful.
You have just experienced
one of the most memorable moments
of your life.
Silence has been revealed to you
as a powerful opportunity
to change
and grow.

You Are a Blessing

If you are a victim of self-loathing,
you are destroying yourself.
You feed your beautiful self
with low-esteem,
fears,
and harmful thoughts.
You feel miserable,
unwanted,
unseen,
unloved,
unworthy,
unappreciated,
unvalued.
You have experienced
so many near-death moments.
You have suffered long enough.

It is time to stop.
It is time to save your true self.
It is time to heal.
It is time to slowly start to heal.
Do justice to your soul
and stop going down that spiral.
Renew your mind.
Renew your heart.
Your true medicine is prayer.
Pray to God
to lead you out of that abyss.
Take responsibility for your life.
Embrace the healing journey
as a blind person would love
to see a sunrise.
Trust yourself.
Plant love in your wounds
and carry hope
in the depths of your heart.
You are so kind and precious.
A heart as loving as yours
is rare to find.
Believe in yourself.
Look at your soul
with the eyes of hope,

and give self-love a second chance.
Or, maybe a third chance,
if that is the case.
Don't let depression
steal your aspirations.
Don't let trauma
kill your inner child.
Your mission in life is to thrive.
Discover your beautiful uniqueness
and offer it to the world.
You are a gift,
a blessing,
a flower.
Discover your inner beauty
and worth.
Heal your soul –
it will help you see your inner world
and the outer world
through the lens of gratitude.
Embrace your precious self
and embrace the healing journey –
it will help you live freely.
Strive to mark your life with peace,
love,
and joy.

You are a gift,
a blessing,
a flower –
try to remember that daily.

Be a Soft Whisper

In a world of hate, noise, and revenge,
choose to be a whisper.
A whisper of love.
A soft balm of healing.
A beautiful song of hope.
A sublime poem of peace.
Choose to become different.
The world is not your master.

The Best Version of Yourself

Never stay in the womb's pain.
Try to exit.

Give birth to the best version
of yourself.
Never let pain hold you captive.
Push.
Scream.
Fight.
Free yourself
from that cage of suffering
and darkness.
You are a giver,
so give birth
to your most authentic self.
You are meant
to make a contribution
to the meaning of a changed life.

Loud Answers

'How are you doing?'
a friend asks you.
Be brave and answer
with all your heart,
'I am still healing.
I am still doing
what I need the most.
I am trying
to reduce the damage
of my past trauma.
I still hope
that everything bad
from my past
will fit inside one small scar.
I am still healing.
That's it.'

A Solitary Art

Healing is a solitary art.
You go inward,
take the most beautiful brush,
dip it in your hopes,
and paint your soul as freely
as only in your dreams you dared.

There is no greater mission,
no other experience
more transformative
than emotional healing.
Dedicate to it your time and energy.
Don't use your imagination,
but the power of self-love.
Paint your soul with the colors of
kindness.
In the end,
you will not admire an artwork,
but a glorious flower –
you.

Talk with Me

When your suffering is so loud
that it covers all noise pollution around
you,
take a deep breath.
I know
it is disheartening.
I know
you hear the sharp cracks
of your heart
getting wider and wider.
I know
you have only one wish.
'Could someone talk with me,
so I stop hearing the disaster
that happens inside me?'
Listen to me.

If there is no one to talk
with you,
be the first who talks
with your soul.
If you cannot talk with yourself,
allow God to speak with you.
Don't sit passively
on the edge of your wounds
and look into the abyss
of your suffering.
Fight for your emotional well-being
and your inner renewal.
Whoever you are
who reads these lines,
take comfort in knowing
that I have been
at this point of life too.
And I healed
and moved forward,
and so will you.

Make Time to Heal

Have you ever asked yourself,
What is my purpose in life
after healing my wounds?
Don't tell me about a better job
or exotic vacations.
They don't offer anything.
They only tell me
that you didn't heal your thoughts yet.
Tell me
about something meaningful,
beautiful
and soul-fulfilling.
Do you plan to offer
your healing gifts
generously
to those who need them?

Do you want to feel helpful?
If your soul is truly healed,
you can no longer live just for yourself.
Ask yourself,
'How can I support others
in their healing process?
How can I soften
someone else's suffering?
How can I help others to rise again?'
If your needs for connection
and compassion
are unmet,
pray.
Prayer is the invisible hand
that always helps.
Have a healing word
on your lips
and in your heart;
you never know
when someone needs that sweet word
and you have it to give away.
Show your smile;
a healed person like you
should never suffer a shortage
of positivity.

Be gentle;
it is so easy to walk in grace
and treat others dearly
and respectfully.
Cultivate the radical love
that keeps healing you and others too.
There is no end to true healing.
Be good,
for goodness can save others.
Spread your inner beauty
in the world,
for the world needs your grace.
Dedicate time to putting your life
on the line with these beliefs.
Please make time to help others,
for their time to heal has come.
It doesn't matter
as long as you can make a difference
in the life of others.
Avoid vanity.
Be modest,
loving,
meek,
caring,
and helpful.

People need to heal
through empathy and love.
You know that.
Give them your treasures.
Show your empathy and compassion.
Help people feel safe and encouraged
in their restorative endeavors.
Be honest and warm-hearted.
Heal others through your love
and affection.
If you do all these things,
you will get the answer
to your question,
What is my purpose in life
after healing my wounds?
Say the answer out loud,
For the rest of my days,
I want to live a healing life.

There is No End

There is no end to deep healing.
Every day,
you can improve something
in your heart.
Address negative thoughts
that bother you.
Cleanse your mind
from stressful ideas.
Heal your words
by adding more positivity
to your daily lexicon.
Refrain from criticizing everyone.
Go deeply inward.
Focus on your soul
and its secret life;
there is always so much to do.

Stay present
and pay attention to everything
that stops you
from changing yourself.
Prune away emotional toxicity.
Every day,
keep healing your heart.
There is no end to beautiful growth.
The more you heal,
the more you realize
that there is no end to deep healing.
And that is the beauty
of being a strong soul, after all.

Dear Reader,

Thank you very much for reading my poetry book. I put all my heart into these uplifting poems to help you heal and fight for your precious soul.

Please take a moment and show your appreciation by writing a brief review on the website where you purchased this book. Other readers might find your thoughts helpful.

And don't forget: wherever you are on your healing journey, allow my poems to hug your inner self. My words will remind you, 'Don't let your light diminish.'

With love,
Alexandra

About the Author

Alexandra Vasiliu is an inspirational poet and the bestselling author of *Healing Is a Gift*, *Healing Words*, *Time to Heal*, *Dare to Let Go*, *Blooming*, *Magnetic*, *Be My Moon*, *Through the Heart's Eyes*, and *Plant Hope*.

As an award-winning poet, she uses her imagination to write books that help people overcome life's adversities, heal their emotional wounds, become stronger, and love again. Her poetry touched thousands of people, one heart at a time.

Alexandra double majored in Literature and French for her undergraduate degree before pursuing her Ph.D. in Medieval Literature. When she isn't busy writing, she can be found browsing in libraries and bookstores, outdoors chasing violet sunsets, exploring pine woods, or spending time with her family at the beach.

Get in touch with her on Instagram @alexandravasiliupoetry and Facebook @AlexandraVasiliuWriter. Or visit her at alexandravasiliu.net. She loves hearing from her readers.

Made in the USA
Las Vegas, NV
15 November 2023

80828359R00134